The Kraków Egg

Pru Kitching

ARROWHEAD
PRESS

First published 2009 by:
Arrowhead Press
70 Clifton Road, Darlington,
Co. Durham, DL1 5DX
Tel: (01325) 260741

Typeset in 10pt Laurentian by
Arrowhead Press

Email: editor@arrowheadpress.co.uk
Website: http://www.arrowheadpress.co.uk

ISBN 978-1-904852-23-0

Printed in UK by
Juma Print, Sheffield, England

for The Ancients
with my love and respect

Acknowledgements

Welcome to the Night Café, Hangout of the Lonely and Desperate is stolen from Simon Schama, from his programme about Van Gogh in *The Power of Art* television series. I should like to thank him.

Baltic Journey in Winter 1992 was longlisted for the 2007 Bridport Prize.

A Russian Professor of Spanish Theatre Goes Abroad, Reasons to get Up in the Morning, Anasazi, I Loved a Bulgarian, Swings and Roundabouts, Ghazal, published in *Love in Vane (Vane Women Press).*

Limestone, What's it Like Up There?, Quarry, published in *Collecting Stones (Vane Women Press).*

Cover Photograph:
Synagoga Stara Kraków by night.

Contents

Welcome to the Night Café,
Hangout of the Lonely and Desperate

so, Vincent, you saw fried eggs in the sky

your Sower floats on a high-wattage sun
your Potato Eaters, trowelled and dug, eat their dusty spuds

black crows in wheatfields of writhing brilliant paint
come   or go   break the rules   are not mad but new

you paint like a clod your deeply sane pictures
dense   clotted   murky things

there is nothing still about your still lives
or the swirling oceans of paint in your self portraits

Louis V greens   soft pink   blood red   harsh blues
the Postman's *check me out* yellow jacket

desperate for your fix of chrome yellow
you consume colours like absinthe or wine

and the drinkers in the night café are ready to destroy
go mad, commit a crime or die

my dear Theo I am not mad but suffering

so the Indus meets the Kabul

and so they meet, I remember, in a straight, milky line
and so the milky line seems to be a permanence
and so this permanence is really just an illusion, like a mirage
and so the Mirage flew high and strong
and, so high and strong   head and heart   is what they said I had to be
and so, what they said, I was, amid the wreckage
and so the wreckage stayed for years and years and no-one dug
and so, after ages, someone cared and dug down deep
and, so they found me and all my rage

Only Once in Two Weeks the Clouds Lift Over Kanchenjunga

at 4am I'm suddenly awake

in the Himalayan Hotel near Kalimpong
not even the ceiling fans stir the April air

there is something

my antennae twitch insect-like
I wonder if I am metamorphosed as Kafka wrote it

something

light   moon light   in through the windowless shutters
            have a look

take care to check sandals and floor for the crunch of cockroach
(here they are as big as Havana cigars)
tiptoe to the window   have a look

a sort of magic

the snow capped triangular peak exposed
as promised in the hotel brochure
has broken cloud cover to stare right back at me
a provocative, domineering lover

time to wake the others

La Mer

Ask about the sea and I'll say
that for me
it's Charles Trenet and it's Debussy.

It's *Peter Grimes,* Virginia's lighthouse
William Turner, *The Shipping News*
a Chagall window's greens and blues.

It's Beethoven by the Bay of Bengal,
it's a raga, it's Neruda
and it's *Crossing the Bar*.

Ask about the sea and I'll say
that for me
it's the Gozo ferry and The Falkland Sound

Rapa Nui rafting and the Old Man of Hoy
a rockhopper penguin
and a Farne Island seal

candyfloss and donkeys and sand and buckets and spades
and *Brighton Rock* and Blackpool Tower
and *Monsieur Hulot's Holiday*.

Ask about the sea and I'll say
that for me
it's Charles Trenet and it's Debussy

Composition in Grey and Blue

(Portrait of Benjamin Britten and Peter Pears by Kenneth Green, 1943)

the one with the nose
and straight black hair
looks intently
at the curly headed one
who concentrates on
what's singing
        winging through his mind

you show their serious love

overlapping shoulders
hint at intimacy
blue jacket presses into khaki

does Ben notice
or is he thinking of another Peter
fighting his demons
and the waves of a Suffolk storm

Baltic Journey in Winter 1992

I was the only passenger to cross what I supposed was tarmac
mysteriously secreted over night under a crisp white film

as if from habit its true nature should be kept from me
the suspicious lone oddity wrapped in wool against the Riga cold

to the icy metal steps and up into the propeller-powered Twin Otter craft
no longer paternally cared for but free to fly, with me and no-one else on board

but a pilot and mate and a cabin crew of three who plied me assiduously
and in equal turns with cola not Coke and orange juice devoid of vitamin C

I wanted vodka the real thing to warm the bones and stiffen up the sinews
for take-off on snow   on ice   in isolation   in expectation   anticipation

and the illogic of naive elation to be historically there where
the Russian Bear had just had its teeth pulled its savagery equalled

by western greed the moral-high-ground-weed of democracy
but I was in love with Chekhov   Tolstoy   Gorky   Dostoyevsky

en route for Moscow where there was power but not bread, not much eating
skid-landed in Vilnius sober and separated from all forms of heating

and found through frosted breath and thawing minds a Lithuanian wassail
a welcome warm with kindness   interest   sweet cakes   spiced ale

A Russian Professor of Spanish Theatre goes Abroad

(For Vidas Siliunas)

Frankly speaking I would rather be eating a good sandwich
is what you stage-whispered into my ear at the theatre in Monterey
where we cringed and squirmed as we watched the play

and your prickly moustache twitched with a life of its own
like an agitated baby grey squirrel and we both giggled so
that we had to leave in disgrace halfway through the show

we were supposed to critique the very next day.
And later that night you reported winning a fight you'd just had
with some *thing* in your cupboard, a creature you clobbered

from considerable height with the *hugest book* you'd happened to borrow
from the library in Moscow and brought all the distance on Aeroflot
with no weight restrictions, no food, compulsory disinfectant.

I think you left that book and its grisly secret
it did not re-appear at *La Cueva* in Mexico City
where macho Francisco and Gerardo, who died,

en you called their little dog
you son of bitch for nipping your leg. To Mexico from Reykjavik
via Calderón de la Barca   Rachmaninov Vespers   Lorca

Kahlo   Rivera   La Grande Place   Lenin   Stravinsky   Kazincbarcika
Liverpool   Copenhagen   Rome   tawdry Monaco   shared minds   quick wit
reminders of a thing squashed dead under a massive borrowed tome.

ERRATUM   Page 13   Stanza 6

laughed until all of us cried when you called their little dog
you son of bitch for nipping your leg. To Mexico from Reykjavik
via Calderón de la Barca   Rachmaninov Vespers   Lorca

How I Identified Myself With a Hot Damp Squid

The restaurant is expensive, the invitation an honour
and this is my second visit though I am reluctant

to sit cross-legged on a low cushion on the floor around a sunken table
dominated by the vast glass-domed dish.

Han Sang-Chul blows cigarette smoke over me
instructs on the art of eating sticky rice
looks away whenever our eyes meet
does not move his knee when it touches mine.

He pours wine, drinks, offers me his chalice, takes mine
in a ritual of respect I do not understand at the time.

My bum is numb, my legs in cramp.
I shift wriggle writhe adjust re-adjust;
under the glass dome the large calamari moves its tentacles slowly
over onion and potato through the seasoned water.

Han and I toast our *kampeis*, my knees locked in spasm,
I see in his eyes the lighting of the fire.

I tackle kim-chi with slithery chopsticks
swallow with difficulty, talk to Bo-Mi and Mr Lee in turns
try not to see the frantic thrashings as the water boils.

In five minutes all is still; the squid and I at peace.
Mr Park slices, Han gives me rice, I take my bowl, my chopsticks – eat.

The Kraków Egg

Walking back from the *Kazimierz* in snowy dark
a bowl of borscht warms my belly   vodka heats my heart
I smell of cigarette smoke   raucous jazz notes bounce my brain

it's a short cold step to the *Stare Miasto* apartment
scene of the day's first meal
a breakfast, I reflect, of philosophical possibility:

the broiling saucepan   life's maelstrom   receives two eggs
the first comes out early, against all egg-rules
has perfect firm white and soft soldier-ready yellow

the second takes longer   carefully timed   removed at the *ping*
is a salmonellery watery mess fit only for the bin

the Kraków egg   as I remark to Jean
breaks the rules   goes against the grain   is contra flow
but delicious all the same.

Home Thoughts From A Broad

Jonathan Joseph is out of town
his brownstone apartment
laddered between Columbus and Amsterdam
is mine for my first time here

he calls from Chicago   the show's going good
the soprano's a babe   the baritone swell
the orchestra's cool   its leader a dude
he's left me a message   he hope's all is well

Jonathan Joseph hangs up the phone and alone
I eat an onion bagel   read his note:

don't go here   avoid going there
never do this especially at night
the subway's ok but only in day time
try to be streetwise and you'll be just fine

Jonathan Joseph used to speak English
but living away has fractured his language

I feel very foreign, against expectation
sigh for my home life   conversation that's easy
am nervous of leaving the Manhattan sanctuary
of asking for one thing and getting another

Jonathan Joseph's away all the week hob-nobbing with Verdi
a mezzo who's Greek   designer from Italy   polyglot band
a chorus that ranges from straight to oblique
and a Russian conductor with drama-queen hands

I eat my burger, my cola and fries   long for a warm beer
steak pudding with kidneys   *Test Match Special*   my dog

Keeps Raining All the Time
(for G.W.)

Don't know why
I thought of you today,
except that the rain
pounds on my skylights
like your fingers did on the piano lid;
and I remember Ronnie Scott's
and that other place you took me to
for the first time.

There's no sun up in the sky
to obscure the tunes that come to mind
or skew the retrospective view.
Rehearsals for a gala show,
it's Anatevka in Glasgow,
Chagall pictures, staying late
in a tenement flat,
a lifted hat in Kensington Gate.

Stormy weather.

Hyenas

their yellowed teeth bared in wheel-clamp jaws
a small gang of urban thugs scours the stinking heaps
for bits of the sick, the old, the almost dead
and dares the watcher to try and jump the queue

they slink and cower in Heep-like feigned submission
malevolent as the Janjaweed, malodorous as skunk or athlete's foot
they share a joke with clawed high-fives, chilling cries
and grins which do not reach the eyes

with their *come on, take me on,* their scornful, tauntful
get close enough to stab me, near enough to bag me
they own the streets, the parks, the corner shops, the day, the night
they fill the air with menace, madness, greed, disquiet

all shifty, furtive, corrupt with rage
they move with ease from veldt to cage, to alley, to town
the coup complete, resistance done
and the watcher knows his world is gone

Rough Guide

No door to this room; a curtain
and then the open air.

On the table by the chair a brochure,
glossed and other worldly,
'One Hundred Best Restaurants in New York –
a Guide.'

The sun sinks like a light switched off;
finding the water pot is hard in the dark,
like raking through soil for fragile shards;
the outside noises crowd in -
animal, alien, alarming -
take charge

in the corner, a baseball bat relaxes
spent, bored, bloody

shapes and shadows, silhouetted against the moon.

You tell me it is time to leave
but I, I am rooted here,
stuck with the possibilities,
afraid of the consequences,
goaded into inactivity.

Portrait of Doña Rosita Morillo by Frida Kahlo

I fear that I will never be finished,
never whole or complete.
Your brown eyes - distracted, wistful -
no longer focused on me,
your piece of earth-purple knitting,
raised mid-row above your knee.

Your white head
bedded in pink-flowering creepers,
your body fixed by shawl and chair;
my fabric, pierced from two sides
by slim silver shafts, grown
as much as it will be.

I will never embrace a human form.

You, like the single cactus
which rises phallus-like behind you,
barbed by life. prickly, defended
will never smile your welcome
to a soft interior.

Johnny Rook

as the caracara flies it's a long way home for you
over tussock grass and diddle-dee; past
rockhopper, magellanic, macaroni, gentoo

did you admire the black-browed albatross; were you watched
by rock cormorants as you scaled these cliffs; did turkey vultures
oversee your miserable fox-hole, wait for you to starve

Johnny, José, Juan - was that your name? – rookie
your plimsolled feet, modest requests for Kit-Kat and Cadbury
museum-displayed for those who will to see

silent cairns on rocky headlands tell where
Tommy   Taffy   Jock   Paddy   Argie   fell at Fitzroy
Goose Green   Darwin Cove   San Carlos Bay

Rapa Nui

I

Hanga Roa

Newcastle to Easter Island via Santiago and Mount Pleasant
the LAN Chile ticket says   you couldn't make it up

in Madrid we collect Mr MacKenzie, who sits next to me
chats away about fish and their parasites

until even he is quietened by Atlantic vastness
the Andean Cordillera, as we descend to Chile.

Excitement almost makes me sick but I've left my gut
in that Condor-swoop down from the Andes

an endless jagged white-topped fearful wilderness
and the film they showed was *'Alive!'* No way.

I'd be dead, I say to Ken   the one who gets eaten
I'd not survive: I'd be baked, grilled, fried.

We scatter llama   guanaco   alpaca   sweet shy vicuña
as though we really are a bird of prey

and land in the land of Bernado O'Higgins
Neruda   Isla Negra   Pinochet   Cabernet.

A change of crew, a flick of the loo, and drunk
on the wine of anticipation it's goodbye to Ken

as we take off again for five more hours flying west
towards a dream   a speck in the Pacific

towards volcanoes   lava   lavish Polynesian fruit
giant basalt figures guarding every headland

and the runway at Hanga Roa, built long by NASA
to accept heroic returning Apollo flights.

II

Moai

You are not as Heyerdahl found you but upright
huge, impassive; arms clamped to attention
at your sides, coral eyes restored to their sockets
empower your collective stare
away from the tumultuous blue Pacific
inland.   You oversee the island
from the burial mounds
of the great clan chiefs you represent.

You do not smile, have no mate
no female forms to join your rigid state
along the Rapa Nui coast.   No fun?
No joy?   If not gods of Egypt, India, Greece or Rome
who *do* you worship? Who looks down
presses your buttons, smiles, frowns
wags a finger, plays your music
beats your drum, lets you dance to his tune?

You lava giants, who wears the topknot?
Who sits highest on the ahu
whose ears are longer, nose flatter?
Which pitted face in rows of faces
carries the authority of history?
Which of you fought well in battle
survived the famine, saw with rock clarity
the end and then enduring mystery?

III

Cult of the Birdman

How do you know, cave dwellers of Orongo,
    I am my master's hopu, his stand-in
        Stupid people! From the crater of Rano Kau
that Makemake wants my egg, my child?
    mine is the honour to dive   to swim
        defiled with your petroglyphs of long beaks
Why will you risk death for it, dive deep,
    to Motu Nui   take the egg from the sooty tern
        egg-clutching bird men, I watch your yearly ritual
swim hard and strong to steal my new-laid
    in his name, for his credit, his year of status
        and laugh at you for thinking it pleases me
from under me   climb the cliffs with it in your teeth?
    his place on a prime ahu, his back towards the sea.
        will prevent your cult from toppling.

IV

Ahu Ature Huki

All alone, outcast, outpost moai; back to Anakena Beach.
Do you remember being left here, abandoned by your clan?
Perhaps at midnight you leave your ahu, dance to the waves' drumbeat.

Ludu Daw Amar from Beyond

(Burmese dissident writer, died April 2008 aged 93)

I cannot lie
this camera does not interpret me
but shows me as I am   I was

I close my eyes
and turn my head to side
and leave my mind wide open

I bear my pain
carry the weight of my destiny
with a smile and a straight back

I understand
there are no flying fishes in my land
the truth is in my face you see

Reasons to Get Up in the Morning
(For Gus)

Your eyes.
Brown, dark as chocolate dropped in a pool of Golden Syrup,
delicious circles of faith,
bitter sweet as a sharp espresso.

You against my legs;
patient pressure, a promise and a poignant knead.

Your rich seductive hello,
reverberating Sarastro-like and warm
as gently heated eucalyptus oil
while we dance and sing
to the tune of *In The Mood.*

The residue of bouillon cube after our kiss;

the Merlot smell of you   sandalwood   saffron,
the maleness persists.

The sixth sense   in-synch   instinct of you
lingering in the chaos when you cease to exist.

Anasazi

(for Mum and Dad)

handprints pressed into red clay
the swastika as symbol of peace

you whom, with love, I call The Ancients
display other traces in another world

pipe, Walnut Plug, Swan Vestas
scruffy envelopes with scrawled-on notes
an *I Love My Dad* badge, a Scouter's leather woggle
a pencil sharpener that used to play *In the Mood*
a ram's head letter opener
a clay ram's head from the Middle East
two clay sheep, one clay sheep dog, a clay lamb
a dog's collar disc.

Eastex clothes *for the shorter figure*
a lucky perfume bottle long emptied of *l'Aimant*
airforce wings in marcasite
three years' worth of letters not lost in convoy
numbered to show the gaps
ways of doing, ways of seeing, ways of trust, ways of faith
because and because and because

after carbon-dating   a rock-solid diamond joining of hands

Limestone

hard man of the Pennines
you burst from the hills
expose yourself
provocative   intemperate

your skyward cracks
hot breath now cooled
reveal long-hidden jewels
galena   fluorite   quartz

grey stone still too soft
for Rodin or Moore you carve out
your presence without pity
declare your dominance and mastery

emperor of rocks
you will survive the next upheaval
outlive our surface crassness
reign over the land's new rhythms

What's it Like Up There?

above Harehope and beyond the lake is the bleak winter horizon
not softened by snow
dirty green patches sectioned by stone walls
improbably perched on the aggressive slopes
the odd off-white dot of a nibbling sheep

and then the farmhouse   sunk into itself
not Cotswold-nestled but dogged   northern
gritting its teeth in the teeth of a Weardale winter

where are the dogs   people   tractor   landrover?
hiding from the grimness of subsistence?

a life different from Ruth and Herbie's
whose cottage down near the wooden bridge
wobbles with each wagon to-ing   fro-ing   going
from quarry to kiln and endlessly back again

different from Lenny Burrup who see-saws out and in
back and forth with sandwiches   pop   a bit or a drill
for the open-cast packers   the movers and shakers
the gelignite drillers   society pillars

what is it like up there   above the explosions
away from the grit the grime the lorries' vibrations
the cordite taste   the rising smoke   the dusty waste
and Ruth and Herbie falling off their chairs

Quarry

beneath the sand, inside the pit
                    I am fugitive

under the shifting surface
I am sand flesh over the bones of a life

if you probe   poke   sift
slip me through your finger sieve

you might find my heart

do not dive in but take the slow and fickle path
towards my submerged pieces

move them and I am re-arranged forever

chase the shards, find the bits
recognise them

reform me if you dare

20th December 1989 at 0946 am

(for Colin Pearson)

afterwards you told me
it was the worst thing you'd had to do
that telephone call from you to me
where you spoke a couple of words
and I   in panic   filled in the gaps
like we were recording a cliché-ridden
episode from a badly-written soap

afterwards you told me I howled
like a wild, wounded animal in pain

afterwards you remembered some London party
where I was with Boot
remembered we each wore a velvet trouser suit
mine dark brown, his deep plum

the colour was important

afterwards I learned to know
the uncommonness of your work
the wings which carried it out of the ordinary
the glazes the textures the colours which flew
in the face of what was expected

and afterwards I eat from a plate which has your mark
pour coffee into cups I will never load into a dishwasher
look at the pink and turquoise and white
which sit on my shelves

and remember a last gooseberry Sauvignon in Islington with Leslie.

Swat Valley Emeralds

A double strand of glittering green chips, unsecured by a cheap gold clasp
worn only once before today (I don't get out much now)
they caress my neck as the eyes of the man who gave me them
and an illicit glass of whisky in the only hotel near Swat,
which he owned, and where I dined alone and conspicuous.

I don't want to take them but am flattered by his insistence
so put them on   aware of his watching distance   his wary drinking
and slowly eat my chicken jalfrezi, peshwari nan, cleansing mouli
and wonder what he wants, this man, this attractive man,
this whisky drinking beard with beautiful brown eyes.

Nothing more than to find me out   discover me, not lover-me
why am I there   why am I alone (oh, why?)   who am I   who would I like to be
(oh, who indeed?)   where will I go next and when will I go there
is my hair really so fair   what is my age and what (ah, what?) is my name.
He offers me his protection   his loneliness   his heart's flame.

In the morning the magic is gone with the night, gone with the light
gone with the empty bottle into the chilling Swat Valley air
a solitary spicy breakfast, no sight of him, only waiters' following eyes
emeralds packed   bags in the van and the driver in place I leave without goodbyes
for Peshawar   a permit to pass   an armed guard for whom I buy lunch.

In the silent passages of Lundi Kotel I can buy hashish   Afghan notes
Kalashnikovs
to smoke, bribe, fire my way past the lorries and bends and lorries and bends
to the top of the Khyber Pass where there is no Kenneth Williams or Sid James
but a Japanese tourist carrying on and hardly less conspicuous than I.
We wave and the green of his eyes takes me to the jewels I was given without
condition.

A double strand of glittering green chips, unsecured by a cheap gold clasp
worn only once before today: I don't get out much now.

Ghazal

(for Iftikhar Arif)

Big questions sometimes are answered by the river.
Did we love when we collided by the river?

Is our love made holy, are our friendships blessed and
is our existence sanctified by the river?

Like the salmon rising, fighting against the flow,
I flail, out of depth, in the tide of the river.

Who knows the secrets of a heart, of a passion;
a soul or a mind, when it hides by the river?

Can fate be eluded, must derangement prevail?
And who must decide? You decide; you, the river.

Will indecision, Hamlet-like, destroy, wreck, claim
innocents; Ophelias; brides of the river?

Would it matter, then, Vedra, mighty and vengeful,
if calmly and cleanly we died, by the river?

Caravanserai

let me lie down with the beasts of burden: camel, donkey, horse, ass
let me sleep in rough hay, wake smelling of ruminant dung and sweet grass

in the hammams of Aleppo rub my burning bones with oils of olive, mint and rose,
bergamot and cinnamon spice; caress me with incense and musk

wrap me warm in Chinese silks and braid my hair with pearls of the Orient,
bartered in Bukhara's souks for rhubarb, saffron or ginger root

entertain me in inner courtyards, where fountains dance to the shenhai and tambour,
lullaby me with Sufi music; suckle me on sherbet drinks and Muscat grapes

with coloured glass and the tiles of Isfahan feast my eyes to peacefulness;
buff the brass lamps to shining splendour; paint my tiredness in tones of tenderness

heal this mind with infusions of poetry; words of the plains and deserts
rhymes of the mountains, snow and heat; rhythms of a lover's heartbeat

with calmness stroke and nourish me; set me on my journey once again.